Flashes of
Thought

United Arab Emirates

القـمـة الحكوميـة
THE GOVERNMENT SUMMIT

Published by Motivate Publishing

Media One Tower, Dubai Media City
PO Box 2331, Dubai, UAE
Tel: (+971 4) 427 3000, fax: (+971 4) 428 2268
e-mail: books@motivate.ae   www.booksarabia.com

ISBN: 978 1 86063 356 0

British Library Cataloguing-in-Publication Data. A catalogue record for this book is available from the British Library.

Printed by Emirates Printing Press, Dubai

Mohammed bin Rashid Al Maktoum

Flashes of Thought

Inspired by a
dialogue at the
Government
Summit 2013

Foreword

It is my pleasure to present *Flashes of Thought*, an important set of insights and reflections by Sheikh Mohammed bin Rashid Al Maktoum.

I very much enjoyed listening to Sheikh Mohammed speak at the Government Summit that inspired this book. In the pages that follow, Sheikh Mohammed expands upon the views that he shared that day and also adds new material with fresh perspectives. It is a diverse book that combines personal experiences with his own ideas about leadership and life.

I was delighted to read the first draft of this book. Sheikh Mohammed, the rest of the rulers and I share a unified vision when it comes to government: its pursuit of excellence, its future, and its role in society. Like brothers, we recognise and honour the teachings of our nation's founding fathers.

As Sheikh Mohammed explains: "The government should work towards the happiness of the people. It is an authority at the service of the people and not an authority over the people."

It was a pleasure for the UAE to welcome more than 30 countries at the Government Summit, and to explore together the pathways to distinction and leadership in government services for citizens.

We must continue to learn from the experience of others, to exchange knowledge with others and to share our own insights with others. After all, it is by focusing on development – and nothing but development – that a nation may achieve sustainable well-being. Development is the driver of prosperity and fulfilment. This has been our focus in the UAE for more than 41 years.

I hope that all readers will benefit from this book. In particular, I say to our youth and to government officials: take this opportunity to learn from a successful Arab leader with many years of experience. God willing, I expect to see the insights of this book applied to the benefit of our nation and to the welfare of every citizen.

Khalifa bin Zayed Al Nahyan
President of the UAE

Introduction

In February 2013 the Government Summit was held in the UAE. It brought together officials and experts from around the world to share creative insights on how governments could make their services more effective, more efficient and more citizen-centric.

I held an interactive question-and-answer session as part of the summit. It was a stimulating dialogue that offered glimpses into a wide range of topics, from management and leadership to personal life, success and its drivers.

It was an opportunity to explain and to reflect. It became, in a way, a defining moment for a range of important ideas – including some that sit at the heart of our vision for this nation. So much so, in fact, that I was inclined to write a book documenting and expanding upon this dialogue.

This book is wide-ranging, as was the session that inspired it. I have included topics that could not be discussed that day due to time constraints, and I have also extended some of my answers.

Last but not least, I would like to point out that I am no scientist. Nor do I claim to be a wise philosopher. This is simply a collection of concise messages, experiences, ideas and thoughts, whose sole aim is to serve our nation and to bring some happiness to our fellow citizens.

We pray to Allah for success in serving our country and its people.

Mohammed bin Rashid Al Maktoum

Contents

الريادة في الخدمات الحكومية
LEADING GOVERNMENT SERVICES

1

At the beginning of my interactive dialogue session at the Government Summit, I asked the audience these questions: Why are we here now? What is the purpose of such conferences and meetings? What is the meaning of our efforts to improve government services? I wanted everyone working in government to look at the big picture: What is the government's job?

My answer was simple and straightforward: The job of government is to achieve happiness for people.

Indeed, our daily work is all about achieving happiness for people.

When governments evolve and develop services to make people's lives easier, they contribute to their comfort and happiness. When governments create opportunities for people, this makes them happy. When governments offer the best education, they equip young people to build their future and so to achieve happiness for themselves. When governments provide excellent healthcare, patients cannot be happier. When governments develop infrastructure, they reduce the amount of time wasted travelling, which undoubtedly contributes to people's happiness and comfort. When justice is served, the whole society is satisfied and reassured.

There is nothing more beautiful than to create joy in people's hearts. This is our aim in developing services, holding conferences and discovering the best government practices out there. We want to make people happy and we ask God to help us in our quest.

When any official puts his mind to this purpose, his days, his decisions, his projects and even his interactions with people will change completely. Even his self-satisfaction will improve a great deal when he knows that he is contributing to the happiness of thousands of people.

This is what we have learnt from our founding fathers, whose only concern was to lead their people from a life of hardship to a new life of comfort and well-being.

Can you imagine that the gross income of the UAE has increased by over 190 times within just 40 years? Also, that there were only 74 public and private schools in the UAE in 1971? Today, we have more than 1200 schools. In 1971 the UAE had not more than seven hospitals; today there are 90 hospitals and over 2000 primary healthcare centres in the public and private sectors. In

> **The government's job is to achieve happiness for people.**

1971 the country had no more than 40 graduates and no universities, but thousands of jobs that needed graduates; today, we have 73 colleges and universities with tens of thousands of students. All of this, and much more.

It is clear to me that the driving force behind our founding fathers' tireless efforts was nothing other than their quest to please people and to ensure their comfort. In this way, our leaders succeeded in building a nation, while elsewhere, established countries were destroyed by leaders driven by different priorities. Our leaders have always aimed to please the people and contribute towards their well-being – and they have succeeded in doing so. That is why the people love them and show them gratitude.

Our citizens are the first, second and third priority! This is the path set for our government by the President, His Highness Sheikh Khalifa bin Zayed Al Nahyan, who is constantly working towards the comfort, satisfaction, stability and happiness of his people.

> **We see the government as an active part of society, never as something that is separate or isolated.**

We could think of happiness as the foundation for many of our ideas and policies. Indeed, some international institutions have even adopted citizen happiness and satisfaction as scientific indicators of development.

We see the government as an active part of society, never as something that is separate or isolated. The government works for the people, achieves its objectives through the people and measures its success through their satisfaction. The government is an authority, but it is an authority at the service of the people and not an authority over them. Its mission is to please them and to build a promising future for their children.

" Our citizens are the first, second and third priority! This is the path set for our government by Sheikh Khalifa. "

2

This chapter sets out our vision for the future of government. Before delving into the subject, however, I would like to point out that when we talk about the government of the future, we focus on the delivery of services and not on political structures. Different countries have diverse forms of government. However, they all work towards one goal: serving citizens.

How can a government be closer to its people, faster, better and more responsive in providing its services? This is my first and foremost concern, and this is the main focus of our development efforts in the UAE.

Some time ago we received a delegation from the Japanese government. They wished to learn from our experience in providing a particular government service: land and property registration. In some countries this is a complex process that can take months or even years. When I told one of my colleagues about the visit, he was impressed by our achievement in creating a system so efficient that advanced nations such as Japan would like to emulate it. "I think you have reached the finish line, Your Highness," he said. "Your teams deserve to celebrate and rest after such a dazzling success."

I disagreed. My recipe for success is continually to raise the bar whenever we reach our goals. It is right to feel proud of such achievements, but we may never feel satisfied. We must always aim higher in order to sustain our ambition and achieve excellence. So I replied: "Our

**Sheikh Mohammed
presses a touch-sensitive
panel during the GITEX
technology exhibition
in 2011.**

definition of success has changed. We must look ahead now to the next generation of governments."

So, what will the government of the future look like?

◈ The government of the future is open for service 24/7, all year round. The private sector remains open for business so why not the public sector? We want our government to be just like an airline – available around the clock.

◈ The government of the future competes with and surpasses the private sector in service quality. We want our government to welcome customers more professionally than hotels; we want our government to manage processes better than banks.

◈ The government of the future is connected. Citizens should be able to complete any government transaction at any government service centre. Integrated service centres will spare citizens long trips from one entity to another.

◈ The government of the future is available everywhere. We want to shift government services onto smartphones so that customers can file and follow up on transactions using mobile devices, at their convenience.

◈ The government of the future is innovative and constantly able to generate ideas. In 2012 the UAE government was able to generate over 20,000 fresh ideas to simplify and improve its services. Our goal is to create an environment that encourages people to generate innovative ideas, implement them and constantly measure their effectiveness. Innovation is the capital of the future.

◈ The government of the future is a smart government with integrated and efficient technical systems. A smart government is so much faster in completing various kinds of transactions.

We have already begun working on many of these ideas and in the years to come, people will start to feel the benefits in their everyday lives. At that point, we will start to consider a new definition for success in providing government services.

" The government of the future is open for service 24/7, all year round. "

3

During my meetings I always talk about positive energy, its influence on our lives and its effect on how much we can achieve. I also mentioned it in my previous book *My Vision*.

I am a believer that all of our actions and accomplishments are simply a reflection of what we bear in our hearts. I believe that positive energy and optimism help us to take up any challenge in life and to succeed in even the most difficult tasks. I also believe that positive energy is contagious: we can transmit it to others. In the same way, we can ourselves be influenced by other people's positivity or negativity.

In the course of my long career, I have seen many colleagues and friends with negative energy that I just could not change. Whenever I would propose any project, they would dwell on its impossibility or difficulty; and whenever I would come up with an initiative, they would just say, "it is not doable." Even if I said that the sun was shining, they would answer that they could not see it; and if I suggested that they come out to see it, they would reply that they just could not do so. Indeed, I have met quite a few negative and pessimistic people. I have replaced them in my life by seeking out much more optimistic, enthusiastic and positive people.

I have faced many challenges in my professional life, but never have I allowed myself to be defeated. Does running water stop when it reaches a rock? Of course not. It turns either left or right, and continues its way. Likewise, a positive person is confident that no challenge will stand in the way of achieving his or her goal.

positive thinking

Start your day with positivity and optimism, with a positive idea and with confidence in your abilities. It will be reflected on your face, in your smile, in your interactions with people around you, and in the way you deal with daily challenges. Haven't you noticed that positive people have a wider smile, a brighter face and a more beautiful spirit? On the other hand, negative people spend their time hiding from challenges and expecting the worst from life.

Positive energy is born of optimism. Our religion assures us that if you are optimistic, you shall find what you seek. If you see the world around you as filled with misfortune, troubles,

> **Does running water stop when it reaches a rock? Of course not. It turns either left or right, and continues its way. Likewise, a positive person is confident that no challenge will stand in the way of achieving his or her goal.**

worries and sadness, so it will be. On the other hand, if you see the world as abounding in opportunity, adventure, happiness, comfort and achievement, it will be that way. It is your mind and your way of thinking that create your reality. You choose whether you want to live your life with positive or negative energy.

Positive energy turns hard times into beautiful moments, hardships into manageable challenges, and the impossible into nothing more than a word or a point of view. It offers you a beautiful perspective on life and arms you with the ambition, drive and motivation you need to succeed.

My advice to all is to arm yourselves with positive energy and to use this energy to raise your team's morale, for a team is influenced most strongly by its leader. Do not undermine your team's morale with pessimism or hesitation. An army's success depends on more than weapons and supplies; high morale can be the key to victory, just as low morale can spell defeat. If morale is high, people will interact with their leader's vision, achieve his or her objectives and follow in his or her tracks. If low morale causes underachievement, the blame will undoubtedly fall on the leader and on no one else. So offer your team optimism and positivity, and they will reciprocate with achievement and creativity.

> **Positive energy offers you a beautiful perspective on life and arms you with the ambition, drive and motivation you need to succeed.**

Sheikh Mohammed gestures to a cheering crowd after his horse won a race in the Dubai World Cup in 2012.

4

A journalist asked me to explain the development priorities of the UAE. I answered in three words: empowerment, education and Emiratisation.

● Empowerment is central to the vision of our President, Sheikh Khalifa. We are currently in a phase of empowerment: we are empowering the citizens of our nation. Human development is an ongoing quest, but today our focus is the empowerment of citizens throughout our institutions and authorities. Emiratis are competent and resourceful. We have great faith in them. They are in control of their own destiny.

● Education is a top national priority and we have launched a number of initiatives and projects in this area. While we are still not fully satisfied with what has been accomplished, education remains our utmost priority.

● Emiratisation, our drive to activate and empower Emiratis in the workplace, is yet another priority for our President, for the government, and for all the emirates and their local governments. The President has launched a set of major initiatives which aim at employing 25,000 Emiratis. We have declared 2013 to be the Year of Emiratisation, and it will be marked by new policies and programmes in this area. I ask all my colleagues in the private sector who have benefited from this generous country to contribute to the efforts of Emiratisation and hence to participate in the development of the UAE.

Sheikh Mohammed works with a student on an iPad at the launch of his 'Smart Learning' initiative in 2012.

These are the most pressing development priorities of the UAE. They also feature prominently in 'UAE Vision 2021', the strategic document that guides our longer-term priorities for the nation. The vision charts a path for every sector in the country, making it an important focus as we work to inform every sector about our specific objectives and expectations. Therefore I have dedicated chapter 19 to 'UAE Vision 2021'.

We have great faith in Emiratis. They are in control of their own destiny.

Sheikh Mohammed speaks during the interactive
session at the Government Summit in 2013.

The victory sign

5

People often ask me the secret behind the unusual hand gesture that I am known to make at moments of personal victory, such as in endurance horse-riding races. Instead of the customary two-fingered 'V' for victory, I raise my thumb, index finger and middle finger together in a three-fingered salute of my own design.

The universal 'V' for victory is traditional elsewhere around the globe, but not for us here in the Arab world. I thought to myself – why should we always express our happiness in the language of others? We Arabs have a deep-rooted civilisation, a rich language and immense creativity.

Therefore, I came up with my own victory sign. I raise three fingers to express three things: 'success' and 'victory' (which are three-letter words in Arabic) and the three-word sentence 'I love you'.

> **We may not live for hundreds of years, but the products of our creativity can leave a legacy long after we are gone.**

Sheikh Mohammed shows his characteristic three-finger victory sign at the Government Summit in 2013.

My victory sign is a simple yet symbolic gesture. It indicates that we should have our own distinct personality, and that we should take pride in our language and our heritage. Creativity should be integral to everything that we do. Creativity should also be intrinsic to our personality, if excellence is what we seek.

I remember more than 12 years ago a work team from a public real-estate company came up with the fresh and innovative idea to build an island in the heart of the sea. Demand for seafront property was high due to its scarcity, so I approved the idea. After some time, they showed me the plans and drawings of the island, which was in the form of a circle. I asked them why they had chosen this shape. They replied that it was the most appropriate and habitual form, and was recommended by experts. I explained that since this would be such a huge project – the biggest man-made island in the world – we should find a way to leave our mark on it. It should not take a common shape. I suggested building it instead in the form of a palm tree. This would symbolise our heritage and also bear witness to an important dimension of our life on this land.

Today, the Palm Islands are world-renowned landmarks that represent something important about us. Their huge

> **To be creative is to add something new to life as opposed to being a passive part of it.**

scale, which makes them visible from space, is a symbol of our ambition, our positivity and our capacity to deliver. Their unique and distinguished shape signifies our spirit of creativity, innovation and heritage.

So, I say to my colleagues: if you accustom yourselves to creativity in small things, creativity on a larger scale will follow. Creativity is inherent in a person's make-up and way of thinking. To be creative is to add something new to life as opposed to being a passive part of it. We may not live for hundreds of years, but the products of our creativity can leave a legacy long after we are gone.

" If you accustom yourselves to creativity in small things, creativity on a larger scale will follow. "

Burj Khalifa

6

A young girl asked me to tell her the story behind Burj Khalifa, the tallest building in the world. This tower is indeed more than just a construction project. It is a story to which thousands of people have contributed and a powerful symbol of progress in our nation.

The drawings that I first received were for an 80-storey tower surrounded by a few smaller buildings, as well as gardens and green spaces. I concluded the first meeting with the project team without commenting on the plans, so the project team knew they would have to do better. They returned a month later with a new plan; still it was not the best.

I told them: "I want the tallest building that man has ever made, on this spot. We want it to be the biggest and the best, with the best gardens and fountains, and with hotels and markets that are also the biggest and the best. We want to build the greatest neighbourhood ever known to man."

Today, Downtown Burj Khalifa is a city at the heart of a city, circled by an avenue that is considered among the most elegant in the world. It offers the biggest mall and the tallest water fountain in the world. It contains grand hotels, luxury restaurants and residential towers home to thousands of people. Downtown Burj Khalifa has become a key landmark for all visitors to Dubai and the UAE.

The tower turned out to be grand and magnificent, so we chose to name it after a great figure, hence the name 'Burj Khalifa', in honour of our President, Sheikh Khalifa.

Foreign officials and the media sometimes ask us why we chose to make it the tallest building. They wonder whether Dubai really benefited from building a tower that cost over US$1.5 billion and as part of an overall project costing US$20 billion. In answer to their questions, I would like to clarify the following three points:

First, building the tallest tower on earth is a national accomplishment, a historic milestone and a key economic turning point. It is a symbol of pride, not only to the Emirati people, but to all Arabs. Four thousand years ago, the tallest buildings known to man were found in our region: Egypt's pyramids were a source of pride and a symbol of the advancement of civilisation. They remained so for millennia until surpassed in height by Lincoln Cathedral in the UK, whose creation marked a new era of civilisation. Today, I hope that Burj Khalifa symbolises the new global changes taking place: a new world where East meets West, where civilisations come together and where human creativity reigns with no heed to geographic, ethnic or religious boundaries.

Thousands of engineers, workers, consultants and others from all over the world worked together to construct this impressive building, and new techniques were used for the first time to reach such heights. This is the United Arab Emirates: a new global hub, where the best minds come together to make the greatest dreams come true. In the

" The UAE is a new presence in the global economy, one as firmly established as Burj Khalifa. "

years to come, the UAE will become increasingly prominent on the world map, because we are well aware that a new era has dawned upon the world. The future is for those who dare to dream and find the courage to pursue their dreams.

Second, we do not seek to derive great economic benefit directly from this building. Rather, its returns will benefit the economy as a whole. Burj Khalifa has enhanced the image of Dubai in particular and the UAE in general, saving millions of dollars on branding. We now have an integrated city with a landmark known and visited by people from all around the world. In 2012, over 65 million people visited The Dubai Mall, part of Downtown Burj Khalifa. To those who remain unconvinced, we say: the greatest risk of all is not to take risks.

Third, building Burj Khalifa sends a message to our people and to the world. To our people, we say that we can achieve so much; we can be number one worldwide in various fields; we can impress the world. We are no strangers to history and civilisation, and we will pay no attention to those who wish to undermine our confidence in our abilities and our people. To the world, we say that the UAE is a new presence in the global economy, one as firmly established as Burj Khalifa.

> ## " The future is for those who dare to dream and find the courage to pursue their dreams. "

Burj Khalifa stands above the Dubai Fountain, surrounded by Downtown Burj Khalifa.

7

'Spirit of the Union' is the official brand for UAE National Day celebrations. Its logo is a stylised silhouette based on an iconic photograph of the seven founding fathers standing shoulder to shoulder at the birth of the nation on 2 December 1971. It is proudly displayed across the nation around that time every year.

For me, this image and the phrase 'Spirit of the Union' have remarkable significance. The idea of 'spirit' is central to the shared identity, common purpose and patriotic unity that sustain and inspire us as a confident and bonded nation.

The UAE is the most successful union in contemporary Arab history. The success of this 41-year-old nation teaches important historical lessons to whoever wishes to draw upon them. The most important lesson is that a union has a spirit. No union can thrive if it is based solely on material interests. We are not uniting companies; we are uniting people.

There must be patriotic feelings that bring together the people of the union under one flag. There must be a team spirit on which to build a common future. There must be complete devotion to the union and to its citizens. Our founding fathers made sure to achieve this right from the very beginning: they worked tirelessly for the union and for all of its citizens.

With God's help, the people of this country have established common values and a great love for their nation, which drive them to work towards a better future for all.

On National Day 2012, Sheikh Mohammed presents to Sheikh Khalifa a gift of the two pens with which their fathers, Sheikh Zayed and Sheikh Rashid, signed the Union into existence in 1971.

In terms of its symbolism, for me the Spirit of the Union represents four essential elements: our soil, our work teams, our flag and our president, Sheikh Khalifa. In other words, teams will only work out of love for their country, beneath one flag and under one president.

My advice to any leader, whether of a country, a company, a team or anything else, is to unite hearts before uniting efforts, and to feel the spirit before building the place. God bless the United Arab Emirates and its people.

" The Spirit of the Union represents four essential elements: our soil, our teams, our flag and our president, Sheikh Khalifa. "

The UAE Cabinet meets on National Day 2012 at Union House, the birthplace of the UAE.

A day in my life

8

A fellow citizen asked me how I spend my day as a person, not as a leader. I replied that I lead a simple life.

On my days off, I start as always with dawn prayers, a habit I highly recommend. Waking at dawn is not hard once you get used to it; it is as if an inner alarm clock rouses you every morning. After prayers, I have breakfast with my family and then I practice some of my favourite hobbies. I ride my bike or go horse riding in the desert. Watching the deer and the rabbits in the wild gives me peace of mind.

I call on friends at their homes, and we go out for lunch in nearby restaurants or for a walk on the beach. Sometimes we go to visit people or go on hunting trips together. My day is simple as is my life, but I am happy with it.

Life was created simple and it is important to live it as such. Simplicity is inherent; it leads to peace of mind and tranquillity. I absolutely do not like to overcomplicate things, as those who are close to me know well.

" Life was created simple and it is important to live it as such. "

We Emiratis are very fond of the sea and of the desert, despite the intense development and modernisation that can be seen in our towns and cities.

The beauty of life is felt in the warm sun shining over the dunes, in the moonlit sky, in the pouring rain, in the green grass growing on the plains and in the valleys, and in joyful gatherings with friends and loved ones. I greatly enjoy the beauty of running horses and am constantly pondering the words of God Almighty: "Do they not look at the camels, how they are made?"

It is such a beautiful life, but many people spend it worrying, burdened and frowning. You can easily see the beauty of life in the laughter of a child, the tenderness of a mother, the smile of a friend or the love of a compassionate wife.

Our founding father, Sheikh Zayed, God bless his soul, was the most down-to-earth of all the world leaders I have had the chance to know. He was also the most smiling and cheerful of all. He loved the beauty of life and sought it in poetry and in prose, on land and at sea, despite his busy schedule and his heavy responsibilities.

My advice to all is to lead a simple life. Simplicity starts in the heart, away from negativity and pessimism.

> **Sheikh Zayed was the most down-to-earth of all the world leaders I have had the chance to know.**

Number One

9

When I am asked about my continued insistence on being number one, despite the difficulty in achieving this objective in all fields, I answer that nobody remembers runners-up. Who remembers the second person to climb Mount Everest? The second person to walk on the moon? In fact, who remembers anyone who comes in second? The answer is: nobody.

We are no less than number one. Whoever convinces himself that he is not worthy of first position has doomed himself to failure from the very beginning. My people and I are fond of being number one.

This is not a new characteristic, but one that we have inherited from our founding fathers. Sheikh Zayed and Sheikh Rashid both loved to be the first and wanted their people to be the first too. From the outset they wished to see the UAE at the very top and their successor, our President, God bless him, is following in their steps.

I am not the only one who wishes to be number one. Abu Dhabi, for instance, aspired to global leadership in alternative energy. It invested, innovated, was chosen to host the International Renewable Energy Agency (IRENA), and created Masdar, a city focused on sustainability. As a result, Abu Dhabi has become a magnet for companies and research centres, and a beacon of innovation in renewable energy.

Abu Dhabi also wished to become a cultural capital of the world. Therefore it built museums, hosted cultural events and embraced the finest works of art in the world. Such is the modus operandi of those who wish to be no less than number one.

We have no alternative to first position. The word 'impossible' is nowhere to be found in the vocabulary of the UAE.

Let me explain why it is so important always to aim for number one. If you want to run one kilometre, you will surely feel tired once you finish. However, if you make up your mind to run 10 kilometres, then you will not feel tired after the first, second or even the third kilometre. Your determination and energy will be proportionate to your goal. Therefore, set a high goal for yourself and do not settle for anything less than the very best. The best is exactly what you will get if you accept no less.

Never ever doubt your ability and never underestimate your capacities. Do not take your mind off your goal. Always work towards first position and trust in God, for it is God who grants success.

Today the UAE is number one in the Middle East in terms of infrastructure, human development, technological development, knowledge economy, citizen happiness and satisfaction, renewable energy, safety, security, trade, tourism, and many other areas. We shall continue our pursuit of global excellence in all fields, for we are a nation that accepts nothing less than first place.

> # The word 'impossible' is nowhere in the vocabulary of the UAE.

Empowering women

10

Some people still wonder about the empowerment of women in our society. Such questions come most often from abroad. My answer is this: we have already moved beyond the phase of empowering women. Indeed, we are empowering society itself through its women; we are empowering our economy by strengthening the role of women; we are advancing government services when women occupy leadership positions; we are launching development projects under the direction of women; we are improving our infrastructure, our health and education services, and even our military by relying heavily on women's roles in these fields.

The strong representation of women in such areas arises naturally from the fact that almost 70 per cent of university graduates are women. This reflects an ongoing process to strengthen the role of women in society. Perhaps this is why we are the top country in the region for gender equality, according to international reports.

Over 65 per cent of UAE government employees are women; over 30 per cent of leadership positions are held by women. I personally could not manage my daily work without women, since 85 per cent of my personal team are Emirati women.

I have said it loud and clear: Beware, men, lest women deprive you of all the leadership positions in the country.

Of course, one of the greatest contributions that women make to our nation will always be their leadership in creating strong and educated future generations that love their country, seize challenges and carry on the building and development process.

When I said some time ago that women are the soul and spirit of the country, I meant every word. A woman has strong feelings, a kind heart, a sharp mind, high ambitions and a refreshing perspective. Women are much more central to Emirati life and to the fabric of our society than many people think. Can a person live without a mother or a sister? Can a house overflow with tenderness without a daughter or a wife? Can a society take any step forward without its better half?

Women are also the very heart of our country. We would never have become what we are today, were it not for the contribution of our loyal, confident and ambitious sisters who are in constant pursuit of excellence and progress, armed with strong will and determination.

I have great confidence in Emirati women and deep faith in their capacities. Their achievements speak for themselves and dissipate any possible doubt in this regard. Some time ago, the Cabinet issued an order to include women in the boards of directors of all companies and government bodies in the country. When people asked me about this, I

" I have said it loud and clear: Beware, men, lest women deprive you of all the leadership positions in the country. "

replied that women represent over half the workforce within these institutions, half the customers of these companies and also half the society influenced by the policies of these government bodies, so is it fair that we men take all the decisions in these institutions on their behalf?

We have read in both ancient and modern history about many great figures educated by their mothers and many great women who left their lasting mark on history. We recognise the greatness of women, both at work and at home. A woman who raises great leaders is herself a great leader. Women have great capacity for generosity, giving and compassion.

There is a saying about rain: it produces abundance wherever it falls. It is our job to provide an enabling environment for women to achieve their highest potential. In other words, we must provide the soil that yields the best harvest from this rain. Our job is to provide an environment that unlocks women's potential – one that protects their dignity and femininity, helps them create the necessary balance in their lives, and values their talents and potential. Given this environment, I am confident that women will perform nothing short of miracles.

> **We have moved beyond the phase of empowering women. Indeed, we are empowering society itself through its women.**

Sheikh Mohammed speaks with a group of young professional Emirati women who are launching their careers as part of a government initiative in 2012.

"It is our job to provide an environment that unlocks women's potential. Given that, I am confident that women will perform nothing short of miracles."

11

I was asked a smart question about horse riding, poetry and leadership, and whether there is a link between them. Of course there is.

Horse riding is synonymous with pride, chivalry, dignity and nobility – all of which are indispensable characteristics for a leader. I have learnt a lot from horse riding and horses. I love my horses and they love me too. Horse riding is a beautiful world and whoever discovers it falls in love with it and cannot stay away.

Our love for horses and horse riding is second nature, and this comes from our Arab roots. I would like to add that horse races, particularly 160-kilometre endurance races, require planning, patience and high control – all qualities that should be found in any leader.

Poetry is another world. A poet's eye is bonded to his heart. The eye and heart of a poet are different from those of others. A poet sees what others fail to see. He scans the sky, the sea and the desert unhurriedly. His look is filled

> **Every leader should have a passion in life that adds depth, uniqueness and style to his leadership.**

with passion and he takes in the beauty of life around him. His heart is very sensitive. He knows his society well, he is touched by its joys and concerns, which he translates into verses full of sincere emotions and poetic feelings. Look at the history of Arabs – we have recorded and passed on our stories in the form of poetry, and we have found that stories told in verse are deemed more sincere and more trustworthy than mere prose.

What I mean is that a poet's knowledge of his society brings him closer to them as a leader. A poet's perception of the aesthetics of life around him is also reflected in his decisions and choices as a leader. Even his projects become lively paintings that speak to people and interact with them, instead of mere rigid projects isolated from the people around them.

Horse riding, poetry and leadership form a triad, positively interacting with one another to make you a better horseman, a better poet and a better leader. Of course, I am not saying that every leader has to be a poet or a horseman; but every leader should have a passion in life that adds depth, uniqueness and style to his leadership.

" The eye and heart of a poet are different from those of others. "

نفود

هبنا من قلبى احبناس

ابنا من قلبى احبناس

لبلها جميع احساسنا

با الطربا

ديباج والماسه

خولها

من جحر ماسه

كرمها

نور نبراسه

Sheikh Mohammed contemplates a poem by a renowned female Emirati poet at the opening of the Women's Museum in Dubai in December 2012.

The Gulf Cup

12

I often like to watch football games with a group of friends. This year our national team reached the final of the Gulf Cup football tournament, and since the weather was so wonderful at that time of year, we watched the match together in a courtyard. The challenge was great and all the Emiratis had their eye on the cup.

I myself used to play football, so I was tense with every move made on the field. I am also a commander, so I was looking at the players as if they were soldiers, and a commander feels a rush of blood to his head as he sees his soldiers on the battlefield. The excitement was palpable and all nerves were on edge.

When the winning goal was scored I jumped from my seat, slammed into the table and ended up with a broken toe.

I had always thought that injuries are only sustained in the field, but there I was injured off the field. However, victory makes you forget your injuries.

When the team visited me after their victory I told them my story and they saw my broken toe.

I would like to add that winning the Gulf Cup or any other championship is an occasion for us to renew our joy and self-confidence, and to join together in shared passions. Winning makes us aware of the importance of team spirit and reminds us that we can succeed if we unite our efforts. It also makes us look forward to the following victory and

Sheikh Mohammed celebrates with the UAE football team following their victory in the Gulf Cup in 2012. Also pictured are his son Sheikh Hamdan, Crown Prince of Dubai, and his daughter Sheikha Shamma.

inspires us to give our very best. I wish our national team ever greater successes in the years to come.

> " A sports championship is an occasion for us to renew our joy and self-confidence, and to join together in shared passions. "

Endurance

13

During the dialogue session at the Government Summit, I was asked about the story behind my success at the 2012 World Endurance Championships, a horse-riding event held that year in the UK. I replied that it was a great honour and took the opportunity to explain what I found meaningful about the experience.

This long-distance horse race was organised in the north of the country in somewhat unstable weather conditions. Participants came from all around the world: USA, UK, Australia, Japan, the Middle East, the Near East and several European countries. There were 150 horsemen from 38 countries in total. The horses were the best and the strongest of their kind. The horsemen were full-time athletes and trainers. All of this added to the tension, especially since I am not a full-time horse rider and practice this sport only as a hobby. Nonetheless, I love horse riding, and I knew my horse and its capabilities well.

I had nominated four horses to pick from and my final choice was one that had never participated in such a large-scale race. I had bought it six years before from a small ranch for a relatively modest sum. I had tried it a month earlier during a small race in Italy, and it was then that I discovered its capabilities. I knew that I could bet on this particular horse because the terrain of the racetrack required a great capacity for ascending and descending mountains.

At the beginning of the race the weather was remarkably unstable, forcing us to cope, in turn, with rain, bitter cold and wind. In an endurance race, you are constantly adapting your plan according to your horse's capabilities, as well as the terrain and length of the race, while trying to keep up with the others. Rushing your horse will tire it, while slowing its pace will keep you behind. If there is a mountain ahead, you should make sure to rest your horse before proceeding; if there is a plain, you can take advantage of the situation to progress, and so on. The challenge lay in balancing all of these variables, but with God's help I was able to come first in this international race, raising the profile of my country and taking home a gold medal.

I would like to draw on my modest experience to give some advice to whoever aspires to attain the title of world champion in any sport, for as people say, it is by teaching others that you broaden your knowledge.

My first piece of advice is to acquire knowledge. You should surpass others in knowledge, for knowledge is the shortest path to victory, even in sports. Know your capacity. Know the capacity of your horse. Know and examine the capacity of your opponents. Know the terrain of the racetrack. Learn its details by heart. Know every part of your horse's anatomy and how it interacts with

" Training opens your eyes to your weaknesses, boosts your self-confidence and brings you a step closer to victory. "

the racetrack. The more you surpass your opponents in knowledge, the closer you come to beating them into second place.

A race is like a battle. Here I quote the famous Chinese philosopher Sun Tzu, author of the military treatise *The Art of War*: "If you know your enemy and know yourself, you will not be imperilled in a hundred battles; if you know yourself but not your enemy, you win one and lose one; if you know neither your enemy nor yourself, you will be imperilled in every single battle." I would like to add: Know your battlefield – for knowledge is more important than capability.

My second piece of advice is training, training and more training. I am not a full-time athlete, but I trained well for this race. I trained my body along the track. I trained my horse to increase its stamina. I trained myself on setting different strategies to reach the finish line. Training opens your eyes to your weaknesses, boosts your self-confidence and brings you a step closer to victory.

My third piece of advice is to trust in God and in yourself, and to be optimistic. These psychological elements are perhaps the most important of all, for they distinguish you from your opponents. Trust in yourself without feeling arrogant or underestimating your opponent. Be optimistic, but do not neglect the smallest details that will ensure your victory. And most importantly, trust in God, for it is God who grants success.

God, of course, knows best about all things. However I sincerely hope that these few words of advice that I have drawn from my modest experience in sports will be of use to my fellow athletes.

Sheikh Mohammed approaches the finish line to take first place at the World Endurance Championships in the UK in 2012.

" **Knowledge is the shortest path to victory, even in sports. Knowledge is more important than capability.** "

My role model

14

I was asked at the Government Summit to identify my role model in life. I replied that it is the Prophet Mohammed, peace be upon him. As for the leaders who have taught me most of what I know, they are undoubtedly the Father of the Nation, Sheikh Zayed, and my own father, Sheikh Rashid, God bless their souls.

From the age of six, I accompanied my father on all his trips. Every European and American city that he visited, I visited with him. Travelling with him was synonymous with learning, gaining experience and exploring life.

I also had the privilege of accompanying Sheikh Zayed on all of his trips after the formation of the Union. These journeys were more like intensive courses in the art of life management, and the methods of leadership and administration. He would teach me not through words but through questions, by involving me in discussions, and through examples. Most often I just observed his actions, his behaviour, and how he dealt with events and people. We have studied in the finest schools and colleges, but I have never found a greater source of knowledge than Sheikh Zayed. He was the greatest of leaders.

Sheikh Zayed had his own view, his own way of facing challenges and his own way of dealing with situations. He handled politics and politicians in his own particular way. He had high values and principles, and also a great attitude. For instance, when former Egyptian President Anwar Al Sadat visited Israel, the Arabs shunned him, imposed a boycott and excluded Egypt from the rest of the Arab world. At that time I was accompanying Sheikh Zayed to a meeting of Arab heads of state, where we met with Hafez Al Assad, who was then president of Syria.

Al Assad was adamant that Egypt must be banned, but Sheikh Zayed argued that Egypt should be brought back into the Arab community. When Al Assad remained opposed and insisted that all Arabs were in agreement on this point, Sheikh Zayed stood his ground. He replied, "Do you think that all the Arabs are with you? Nobody is with you. We should embrace Egypt once again." And that is what happened.

Sheikh Zayed had his own profound political view of the interests of the Arab world. In his approach to such matters, the voices of wisdom, reason and unity always prevailed.

Here I would like to recount an amusing anecdote about an incident during a meeting of heads of state from the Gulf Cooperation Council (GCC). The evening before the meeting, we were sitting with Sheikh Zayed, and it was getting late. I was with Sheikh Mohammed bin Zayed (son of Sheikh Zayed, later Crown Prince of Abu Dhabi) and together we kept trying to make our exit, but each time, Sheikh Zayed would call us back. So we stayed up with him until the late hours of the night. Finally, we escaped in a moment of distraction.

" My greatest role model in life is the Prophet Mohammed, peace be upon him. "

The next morning, I was the first to join Sheikh Zayed at breakfast, as was my habit. I saw that he had written a poem about our behaviour the previous night. It was a clever and light-hearted verse that teased us for the way we had sneaked away.

After breakfast I replied by writing my own light-hearted verse, which matched Sheikh Zayed's poem in rhyme and style, and read it out to him. My poem was slightly suggestive and irreverent.

This whole episode reflects something fundamental about Sheikh Zayed's character. He approached his role as mentor with great warmth, humour, affection and ease. Teasing us by dashing off a line of verse was characteristic of his creative and spontaneous spirit.

May Sheikh Zayed and Sheikh Rashid rest in peace and may God bless their souls. I was one among many to graduate from their school of thought. Today our generation of leaders is the fruit of their hard work and education. A true leader is one who forges great leaders.

" **We have studied in the finest schools and colleges, but I have never found a greater source of knowledge than Sheikh Zayed.** "

Perhaps the most important lesson we have learnt from them is how a leader should be a father to his people. Indeed, Sheikh Zayed and Sheikh Rashid always saw the Emirati people as their children and up to this day, this family spirit still runs in the blood of our country.

> **Perhaps the most important lesson we have learnt from Sheikh Zayed and Sheikh Rashid is how a leader should be a father to his people.**

Time management

15

During the dialogue session at the Government Summit, I was asked how I manage my time to get so many things done. I would like to make clear that credit is due to the thousands of hardworking teams who stand behind our accomplishments. I am nothing more than their leader.

As regards time, I say that we all have 24 hours a day. The question is not how we manage our time, but rather how we invest our time. First, there are plenty of tasks that can be performed in less time. For instance, what can be said in a three-hour meeting can be summed up in half an hour, and what can be completed in one month can also be done in one week. Such a skill is indispensable if you wish to achieve more in less time.

On the other hand, time management should be well balanced, for creating balance in your time entails balance in your life. You should have time for your family, time for your work, time for yourself, time for your hobbies, time for self-development, and so forth.

" Manage your time, know your priorities, enjoy life and leave your mark. "

Time is life, and as such, it cannot be stored or paused. Time is like a flowing river: you cannot step in the same water twice. One of my principles in life is that every minute of our life is worth filling with accomplishments, happiness and good deeds. If you wish to achieve, make the most of every single minute of your life. Never stop working, thinking, innovating and enjoying every single minute, and sure enough, all of this will bear fruit.

Every new day brings new opportunities. Those who do not value every passing minute, every passing hour and every passing day cannot value their life. It saddens me to see young people today spending so much time in coffee shops, watching TV or playing video games, for their time is a great asset to the development and prosperity of our country, society, families and generations.

Some see the year as equivalent to 365 days. Well, I say that a year is equal to the number of days that you have invested in yourself, your family, your society or in your spiritual life. These are the only days that actually count when writing the story of your life. So make the most of them, manage your time, know your priorities, enjoy life, leave your mark and most importantly, never ever allow anyone to steal your time – for by doing that, they would be stealing your life.

> ## Time is like a flowing river: you cannot step in the same water twice.

The Arab Spring

16

Nowadays, the Arab Spring and its repercussions on the region are hot topics at every meeting and summit. However, these issues did not appear overnight. The general feeling of discontent and dissatisfaction that unleashed this wave of transformation had been felt for many years.

During the 2004 Arab Strategy Forum, I remember telling Arab leaders loud and clear that if they did not carry out radical reforms with tangible benefits for citizens, their people would forsake them and history would judge them harshly. I advised them to bring about change or accept that they themselves would be changed.

I was not foreseeing the unseen, for God alone may know what the future has in store. I was simply drawing on lessons from our history, which gave a clear indication of what was bound to happen. For every action there is a reaction, and every incident has repercussions.

I remember visiting some leaders and telling them frankly what was likely to happen. Some of them became angry and replied that none of that was mentioned in their briefing reports. So I said to them, "Your problem lies in your briefing reports. This is my honest advice to you and it is not driven by any motives." I only had the Arab peoples' best interests at heart.

I also reasoned with other leaders, saying, "You took over by revolution and now you need to provide a revolution for your citizens. You should give them something. Your people are ultimately seeking a life of dignity, and you should spend all that you have on them and give them all that you can." Their excuse at that time was that they did not have anything to give, knowing full well that they personally were not short of money.

They thought their people would continue to believe them. You can lie to your people for a year or perhaps for two, but surely not forever. The biggest problem was that they themselves believed their own lies, and forced their press and media to highlight only the positive aspects of the situation. They ended up believing these stories and fell under the illusion that no problems existed. The influence of social media was growing, many truths were being unveiled, and people's patience was wearing thin. The explosion was imminent.

I am in no position to judge the old or new governments of these countries; and I am certainly in no position to judge

"How does history judge Sheikh Zayed and Sheikh Rashid? I personally know many a man whose eyes well up with tears at their memory. Such is history's judgement."

Sheikh Mohammed speaks during the interactive session at the Government Summit in 2013.

their people or their revolutions. My only wish is for people to achieve stability, security, peace and progress. In saying so, I am also voicing the hopes, wishes and goodwill that my country holds towards all Arabs.

People want governments that provide excellent healthcare, education, housing, justice and safety. They want real economic development. This is our singular focus when we strive to provide leadership in government services. Until all governments commit their energy to such principles, unrest and crises will continue to shake our world.

I mentioned at the beginning of this book that a government should work for the happiness of its people. Our nation's founding fathers, Sheikh Zayed and Sheikh Rashid, aimed to make their people happy and to ensure their well-being. They worked tirelessly to reach this objective. How does history judge Sheikh Zayed and Sheikh Rashid? Are they still remembered today? Of course. I personally know many a man whose eyes well up with tears at the memory of Sheikh Zayed and Sheikh Rashid. Such is history's judgement.

I am in no position to judge the old or new governments of these countries, their people or their revolutions. My only wish is for people to achieve stability, security, peace and progress.

17

The UAE has for many years been known as a pillar of stability in the Middle East. Our status as a safe destination for investment is linked to our role as a regional business hub and economic gateway. Recently, questions have been asked about the extent to which we benefit from funds flowing in from Arab Spring countries affected by unrest.

I am bothered by comments in the Arab media about the UAE "deriving benefit from unrest" in other countries. And what bothers me most is the fact that there is no evidence to back up such claims. The UAE is even being described as living off the tensions in other countries – countries that are dear to us and whose stability is our only wish.

First, I would like to say loud and clear that the UAE does not work this way. We rank among the top countries when it comes to helping other nations to achieve stability, prosperity and development. We also rank among the world's top countries in terms of foreign aid as a percentage of national income.

Second, the UAE economy is built on stable foundations. We are developing a model for achieving sustainable development, rather than temporary development that lives off regional tensions. Our country embraces people from 200 nations, all working, investing and giving the best they have to offer. Every year we welcome more than 10 million tourists from all around the world.

Our strategic trade partners do not include any Arab Spring countries. Indeed, none of our top ten partners is an Arab state, apart from the Kingdom of Saudi Arabia. The investments flowing into the UAE come from all over the world and are all published, totalling 30 billion dirhams (around US$8 billion) in 2012. Worldwide investments in the UAE were flowing strongly long before the Arab Spring. They have continued, and will continue, to flow.

Third, real estate and other types of investments made by UAE companies in the Arab Spring countries are far greater than the capital flows that we receive from these same countries.

To those who say that the UAE benefits from regional unrest, I bluntly reply that the UAE would benefit double and triple, were the region stable and free of tensions.

"The UAE would benefit double and triple, were the region stable and free of tensions. "

Ideas and creativity

18

I was asked at the Government Summit about how I come up with so many new ideas and the source of our creativity. Therefore, I took the opportunity to talk about the importance of innovation in government.

The fresh thinking that fuels constant progress in government does not come only from the centre and the top, but from all around and from the roots. Employees must be empowered as a source of innovation. Creative ideas are the fruit of interaction between leaders and their teams.

Military leadership has taught me that a commander must listen to his soldiers. Consultation and collaboration are ingrained in our culture. What better example of leadership could there be than that of our Prophet, peace be upon him, who always took heed of his companions' views?

Ideas come from all kinds of people: citizens and residents, children and adults, officials and employees. Everyone contributes ideas, no matter how simple. I have the habit of asking everyone I meet to provide me with fresh ideas that may contribute to our development.

I will digress a little to highlight the importance of creativity. Creativity is the most valuable asset in any public institution; Without it, you can never challenge your past achievements, change your current situation nor surpass others.

Progressive governments embrace creativity. It is the lifeblood of our quest to improve services, advance our people and develop our country. A creative government is a living system that grows and develops. In 2012 the UAE government was able to come up with more than 20,000 fresh ideas. Some of our officials talk about creativity and place suggestion boxes in their institutions, thinking that this renders them creative. It doesn't. In order to produce genuine, meaningful, beneficial change, creativity must become an established culture with integrated systems.

Creativity can never thrive in an institutional environment that does not favour learning and the dissemination of knowledge. Nor can it thrive in an institution that resists change or fails to encourage the clear and transparent exchange of ideas and views. I know an institution that was able to increase its returns by 100 million dirhams (around US$27 million) and to cut costs by 240 million dirhams (around US$64 million) thanks to creativity. The key to this achievement was this: the institution began rewarding employees according to their creative contributions.

I was once asked how to become creative. I replied that we should get accustomed to not getting accustomed. Accustoming yourself to a situation gives you comfort, whereas change requires hard work and getting out of your comfort zone. People are not usually fond of change and tend to fight those who call for it, because it requires them to change their habits. To all creative minds, I say: you will always find someone who will fight your ideas. This will be the first indication that you are on the right track. To all officials, I say: do not fight change – embrace it.

" We should get accustomed to not getting accustomed. "

19

This chapter explains the most important national objectives that we aim to achieve by 2021, the year of our country's golden jubilee.

More than two years ago, I met with my fellow ministers at Qasr Al Sarab Desert Resort in Liwa to develop a long-term vision for the UAE. We discussed our top national priorities and drew up a roadmap for this critical phase in the country's development. An important strategic document titled 'UAE Vision 2021' was developed, based upon the national programme formulated by President Sheikh Khalifa, which places the citizen at the centre of the country's development.

Next, I held a series of meetings with the rulers of the emirates and with many senior government officials. Together we discussed the Vision and agreed to consolidate our plans and strategies towards achieving it. We agreed on one overarching goal: to enable the UAE to become one of the top countries in the world by 2021.

We have every right to dream of becoming among the best countries in the world, knowing that we do not rely solely on wishes, but that we are serious in our ambition to be the very best.

We are no less than any other country. Our capabilities are no less than those of other peoples. Our love for our country is no less than their love for their countries. And we have at our disposal sufficient resources to achieve our ambitions.

To all government officials, I repeat over and over again: trust in yourselves and in your teams, and always have faith that we can be among the top countries in the world.

In the sections that follow, I present the most important national objectives for achieving Vision 2021, highlighting the main fields of leadership in government services where we aspire to come first worldwide. The vision is detailed and available to the public at www.vision2021.ae.

First-rate education

One of the most important lessons from both ancient and contemporary history is that the progress of countries, peoples and civilisations starts with education. The future of nations starts in their schools.

Education is a passion that I share with our President, Sheikh Khalifa, the rulers of the emirates and with Sheikh Mohammed bin Zayed (Crown Prince of Abu Dhabi). It arises from our awareness that the UAE stands no chance of progress without an excellent education system. Improving education is a constant process that has no finish line, because the world is evolving. The sciences are expanding and different tools are being invented every single day. We are participants in a never-ending race, and God willing, we will keep running.

> **We have every right to dream of becoming among the best countries in the world.**

Whoever looks at the development of our education system over the past four decades will notice the giant strides that we have made. Education is a right for all, guaranteed by the constitution. Since the inception of the UAE in 1971, the number of schools has increased 16-fold, the number of students has grown 25-fold, and the UAE has become renowned as a world leader in female education.

In recent years, we have focused in particular on building schools and universities to ensure education for all citizens, irrespective of location and age. In the years to come, we will focus on delivering education in a way that equips our students with modern technical abilities as well as life skills.

Our goal is for Emirati students to rank among the top 20 countries in the world in science, mathematics and reading. I have great confidence in our children and their capacities. They are no less capable than others. There is nobody inherently more capable than them.

We also aim to reach international standards for our education services. We want all our public and private schools to be accredited. Last but not least, we are working towards the certification of every single one of our teachers according to the best international standards. Such are our utmost education priorities.

> ## The progress of countries, peoples and civilisations starts with education. The future of nations starts in their schools.

World-class healthcare system

Let us move on to one of the most vital sectors in the UAE Vision 2021: healthcare. We offer 100 per cent coverage for public health services in all regions. So, our challenge does not lie in providing medical services, but rather in improving their quality.

If we want high-quality medical services, we must not only develop clear standards, but also bind public and private sector employees to comply with them. We will set standards for medical staff, medical services, drugs, preventative medicine and hospital management, among other things.

In this way we will work towards the accreditation of every hospital in the country according to the best international practices by 2021.

Human development

We have a vision for a society characterised by excellence in human development at all levels of education, health, social care and culture. We want the UAE to rank among the top 10 countries on the global human development index. By building families, bringing communities together and strengthening the bonds between their members, we also expect the UAE to rank among the top countries on the global happiness index.

Competitive knowledge economy

Our interest in this sector is very high and so is our international ranking. The reason is simply our strong belief that a thriving economy is central to the life of dignity that we wish to provide for our people. The basic function of government is to make people happy and this is only possible by ensuring a decent life for citizens.

Sheikh Mohammed leads a workshop on his government's long-term plan, 'UAE Vision 2021'.

United Arab Emirates

VISION 2021

الإمارات العربية المتحدة
UNITED ARAB EMIRATES

عام اليوبيل الذهبي 50 GOLDEN JUBILEE YEAR

UNITED IN AMBITION AND DETERMINATION

نريد أن نكون من أف
دول العالم ب

One of the pillars of a decent life is a good income, which is strongly related to national economic performance.

Our economy is characterised by the diversity of its sources of income – a strategy we have successfully implemented at an early stage, setting an example to many oil-producing countries who wish to reduce their dependence on a single economic sector.

Our first economic goal is to enhance our global competitiveness. To continue to grow and develop, it is imperative to look at the rest of the world with a competitive spirit, for the day that we lose this spirit will mark the beginning of our regression. Our objective is to rank among the top 10 countries on the global competitiveness index and on the ease of doing business index.

Our second economic goal is to improve the entrepreneurial sector by supporting small- and medium-sized enterprises, since we wish to empower citizens to start up their own businesses based on initiative, creativity and self-reliance. Most importantly, we need to instil an entrepreneurial culture within our schools and universities. We want to

> **It is imperative to look at the rest of the world with a competitive spirit, for the day that we lose this spirit will mark the beginning of our regression.**

build a generation of hard-working and creative young entrepreneurs with great courage and ambition, as well as a sense of responsibility. All that we can wish is for our youth to enjoy the benefits, for themselves and for their families.

Our objective is to rank among the top 10 countries on the global entrepreneurship and development index (GEDI). We are well aware that many Emiratis prefer employment, and that not every person is cut out to start up his or her own business. Thus, we are working in parallel towards the Emiratisation of the private sector, which annually generates more than 100,000 positions fit for our citizens.

We have declared 2013 the year of Emiratisation. We aim to increase the representation of Emiratis in the private sector 10-fold by 2021. Job security is not a marginal issue for this government; on the contrary, it is a top national priority.

Sustainable environment and integrated infrastructure

In recent years, we have been able to develop our infrastructure up to truly global standards. This has been achievable quickly, in part because material development usually takes less time than human development.

The most recent global competitiveness report ranked the UAE sixth worldwide on the infrastructure quality index. We score highly for airports, ports, roads, mobile phones, and electricity infrastructure. Our objective for the coming years is to rank first on the global infrastructure quality index.

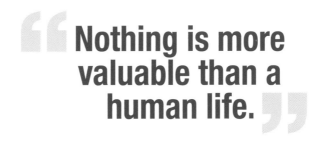

Nothing is more valuable than a human life.

Justice is the foundation of governance; such is our approach in the UAE, a legacy we strive to maintain from our ancestors. Justice in the context of judicial systems does not come only from passing righteous verdicts, but also from the ease and clarity of legislative processes, and speed of resolution of court cases. These are only possible through streamlining procedures, deploying the latest technology in courts, and putting in place the highest standards of transparency and accountability.

We shall continue to develop the judicial system in the UAE based on the principles set out for us by our founding fathers: independence, compatibility with Islam, and mindfulness to human moral standards.

As for the security and safety of the UAE society, I personally get very disturbed with traffic accidents, which have caused us the loss of many young Emiratis, unfortunately. We have provided the best road, bridge and tunnel infrastructure, and most of our young people drive very safe cars. So the main reason behind such accidents is nothing other than high speed and inattention while

The responsibility of development is a heavy one, the road is clear, the clock is ticking and our country will bear witness to our actions.

driving. We aim to rank among the top 10 countries with the lowest traffic-related death rates, because nothing is more valuable than a human life and as such, it cannot be taken for granted.

I have given a brief overview of our most important national objectives towards achieving Vision 2021. I apologise for bringing up such a dense topic in a book such as this, but I am a true believer in people's right to know the roadmap, objectives and priorities of their country. It is in clarifying such objectives that we come closer to achieving them.

The government cannot achieve its objectives alone, but must join forces with society, the private sector and all sections of society. The responsibility of development falls on everyone's shoulders. It is a heavy responsibility. The road is clear, the clock is ticking and our country will bear witness to our actions.

Our country may be small, but our people are remarkable and the feats that we have achieved are amazing. We have no way towards the future other than by joining efforts and working together. So together let us lead our country and generations towards a brighter and more prosperous future.

Our country may be small, but our people are remarkable and the feats that we have achieved are amazing.

Taking risks

20

The UAE is well known worldwide for its remarkable pace of development. When people see ambition and construction on this scale, when they see us launch major projects and plans even amid global economic challenges and regional instability, they often ask: "Don't you find that risky?"

My reply is that no project was ever achieved without risk. Every kind of work entails a certain degree of risk. So, do we stop our life and work? Even banks entrusted with people's money run risks. So, do we stop banks from operating? By going to work by car we are taking risks. By travelling by plane we are also taking risks. So, do we stop going to work or travelling?

Certainly not. Life is full of risks. How can we achieve our objectives, boost our economy and ensure people's happiness if we do not launch new projects and take some calculated risks?

Challenges are omnipresent and so are risks. Whoever perseveres towards his goals will surely achieve them. Whoever comes up with excuses to stop growing will never be short of excuses.

With each new project or idea that we launch, I face the same questions about risk. I always repeat that the greatest risk of all is not to take any risk. It is true that we never launch a project that is not thoroughly examined and researched; however, we refuse to instil fear into our minds and into our teams.

We refuse to magnify the risks surrounding us. We refuse to be hindered from working, building and growing, even with tensions, unrest and wars going on around us. Our region has witnessed three significant wars in the past three decades. If we had waited for stability to be restored before launching our large projects, where would we stand today?

The best response to regional tensions and also to international challenges in the global economy is to work faster and to complete bigger projects than ever. Development favours stability. When economies are less stable, they can be boosted and anchored by large projects.

Our region and its peoples are in dire need of a successful model in the Arab world – one that gives them hope and proves that focusing on growth is far better than focusing on wars; that launching projects is far more useful than launching rockets; and that building the future is only possible by consensus, reconciliation and team spirit.

Every nation can harness the energy of its citizens, either towards constructive work to generate optimism and hope, or towards tensions, unrest and war.

Arabs are smart people and I am optimistic for the region's future, despite all the tensions it is currently witnessing.

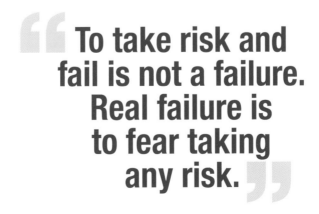

To take risk and fail is not a failure. Real failure is to fear taking any risk.

I would like to move on to another dimension of risk-taking, that is, taking risks at a personal level.

A person who does not take risks in life will avoid difficulties, problems and loss; but he will never mature or learn new things. He will never change. He will never even dare to love. In short, he will never live his life to the full. There is a saying that you cannot discover new oceans if you lack the courage to lose sight of the shore. Life is full of experiences, people, places and adventures; by avoiding risks, you will lose out on all of this.

Quite often we see two people coming from the same background, having received the same education and enjoying the same level of intelligence – but one of them is far more successful than the other. Why is that? It is because one person dared to cement his ideas into reality, to experiment with his innovative side and to transform his life, while the other did not have such courage.

To take risk and fail is not a failure. Real failure is to fear taking any risk.

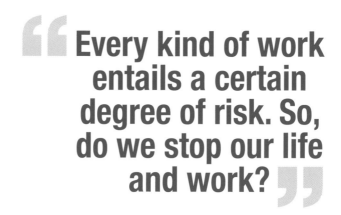

Every kind of work entails a certain degree of risk. So, do we stop our life and work?

Sheikh Mohammed bin Rashid and Sheikh Mohammed bin Zayed (Crown Prince of Abu Dhabi) lay foundation stones for a development project in the Emirate of Fujairah. Also pictured are Sheikh Hamdan (Crown Prince of Dubai) and His Excellency Mohammed Al Murr, Speaker of the Federal National Council (the UAE's parliament).

" If we had waited for regional stability to be restored before launching our large projects, where would we stand today? "

Challenges

21

Life is filled with challenges. The lives of our fathers and grandfathers, and also our own lives, have been this way ever since the inception of the UAE. Growing from a simple country to a global nation did not happen without challenges. Had we ceased to grasp these challenges, our country would have stopped progressing.

In the UAE we have two great role models for stepping up to every challenge that comes our way: Our founding fathers, Sheikh Zayed and Sheikh Rashid. Throughout his life, Sheikh Zayed never failed to rise to a challenge. The greater the challenge, the stronger his determination. Thanks to such perseverance, we have been able to conquer each and every challenge that has come our way. We simply never give up.

The greatest challenge that I have ever faced personally has been convincing my teams to believe in my vision and

> **An easy life does not make men, nor does it build nations. Challenges make men, and it is these men who build nations.**

to trust in the change I seek. Words alone are not enough; it is necessary to succeed a few times in order to reassure people that you are on the right track, and to convince them to embrace your vision.

Great men are defined by the challenges they take up. I personally cannot judge an individual's strength and capability, unless I confront him with a challenge, for challenges bring out a person's best and worst sides. They are also the best tool for refining a team. Just as high temperatures remove impurities from gold, challenges purify the capacities and strength of those who take them up.

Since its inception in 1971 the UAE has faced many challenges, both internal and external, but fortunately God gave us strong and wise leaders who stepped up to these challenges, setting an example for their people.

Every challenge is an opportunity for learning, a chance to test our capabilities and knowledge as well as the character of the people around us. Without challenges, victories and achievements would be meaningless.

True experience is measured not by the number of years that we have worked, but by the number of challenges that we have taken up. I sometimes encounter people who hold

" Every challenge is an opportunity for learning, a chance to test our capabilities and knowledge. "

Sheikh Mohammed speaks during the interactive session at the Government Summit in 2013.

no academic qualifications, but who enjoy great wisdom and a broad mind, and have more achievements under their belt than many others. The reason is that they have taken up more challenges than others, and their feats bear witness to this.

An easy life does not make men, nor does it build nations. Challenges make men, and it is these men who build nations.

> **"Throughout his life, Sheikh Zayed never failed to rise to a challenge. The greater the challenge, the stronger his determination."**

The impossible

22

'Impossible' is a word coined by those who do not want to work, or rather, those who do not want us to work. 'Impossible' is nowhere to be found in the dictionary of the UAE. It is a word used by some people who fear to dream big. It is like chains that tie a person down, hindering his every move. It can confine a person like a great prison, preventing him from moving around, living life and achieving great heights.

We were told that developing a tourism industry in our hot desert was impossible; today we receive over 10 million visitors yearly. We were told that building towers in the sea was impossible; today we have the biggest man-made island in the world with hundreds of towers housing thousands of people. We were told that our region was teeming with tension and therefore our trade could not thrive; today we are the biggest partner in the Middle East for the most important economies in the world. We were told that bringing Arabs together was impossible; today the UAE has proven itself to be a union of unprecedented success.

> **Impossible is a word used by some people who fear to dream big.**

The seemingly impossible is not a gauge of our strength and potential, but rather of our faith in ourselves, of our confidence in our capabilities and of our belief. Do not ever allow the word 'impossible' into your life, because it would mean that you are weak, or that those around you are weak. That said, the truth is that there is no such thing as a person who is strong or weak – only a person who is willing or resistant.

I have no clue who invented the word 'impossible', but it was clearly someone looking for an easy life, a life of sleep and inactivity. We have never had faith in this word. Today I hear the expression 'beyond the realms of possibility'. It is said that there are three impossibilities in life: first, the griffin, a mythical bird that never lands but is always flying, to the point of laying its eggs in the sky, where they hatch into fledglings in flight and never reach the earth; second, the ogre, of which we have never seen any trace, for it too is a myth; and third, a loyal friend. Mind you, these are not my words, and many people have added other impossibilities to this list, each according to his convictions.

Last but not least, I would like to tell you that the impossible cannot be where there is perseverance and faith. There is no impossible in life.

> **" The impossible cannot be where there is perseverance and faith. There is no impossible in life. "**

23

A short while ago I met with a group of around 500 international executives from the biggest companies in the world who came to Dubai for a conference. They asked for a speech, so I told them I would recount three stories that summarise the three most important characteristics to be found in business leaders.

The first story dates back to 1985 in Dubai. An airline controlling around 70 per cent of the air traffic in Dubai Airport asked us to put an end to our open skies policy, which entitled any airline to operate in Dubai Airport. They wanted to protect their market share and even set us a deadline of a few weeks to comply. If not, they threatened to withdraw from the airport, which would lose almost 70 per cent of its traffic.

We refused their request for a simple reason: we believe that competition, and not protectionism, is healthiest for our country. So we rented two aeroplanes and created an

Competition always makes you stronger and better. It is feared only by the weak.

Sheikh Mohammed looks out over Dubai International Airport. Terminal Three, pictured in the background, is the largest building in the world by floor space and the home of Emirates Airline.

airline that we called Emirates. In short, they forced us to establish our own airline, which now ranks third worldwide.

The first lesson to be learnt is that competition always makes you stronger and better. Competition is feared only by the weak. Our country is better because it is open to competition; our employees are better because they compete with everyone; our streets are better because we want them to surpass those of other countries. Even our government institutions become better when we give out distinction awards that encourage competition for first place.

The second story took place in the early 1970s. A group of traders paid me a visit and asked me to dissuade my father from undertaking a project that he had set his mind upon. The project was none other than the Jebel Ali Port.

The traders believed that this project was unnecessary and would only burden the Treasury with huge costs. I spoke briefly with my father, God bless his soul. After a moment of silence, he told me that he was building something for the future, something that we would not be able to build with our future resources. Today, Jebel Ali Port remains the largest man-made harbour in the world and also ranks among the top 10 busiest cargo ports worldwide. It has more than 60 giant berths and a free trade zone hosting thousands of companies. Moreover, our experience in this field has qualified us to run over 60 ports around the world.

The moral of this story is that we should arm ourselves with a long-term vision, high ambitions and far-sightedness. Without a vision to guide our path, and without ambition that knows no limits, we can never build a bright future for generations to come.

The third story dates back to 1999 when we considered building a business zone dedicated to technology companies. We called the project Dubai Internet City. The investment was modest, but the idea grew to include several specialised zones in media and education, and more. Today these zones encompass 4,500 companies

❝ Without a vision to guide our path, and without ambition that knows no limits, we can never build a bright future for generations to come. ❞

Cranes load cargo at Jebel Ali Port. The port handled trade equivalent to 13.3 million containers in 2012.

and 54,000 employees, making Dubai the region's capital of creativity in these domains.

This shows us that creativity and ideas can build countries and institutions. The future belongs to those who generate ideas. Today, the UAE is the only country in the region to have achieved official categorisation as a knowledge-based and innovation-based economy.

Our objective is to rank among the top countries in the world. With the help of a long-term vision, high competitiveness, creativity and innovation, we are sure to get there.

" Creativity and ideas can build countries and institutions. The future belongs to those who generate ideas. "

24

Performance monitoring is one of the most important pillars of successful government. We empower government officials, give them authority and entrust them with budgets. At the same time, we monitor and hold them accountable for their performance. So what happens when an official makes a mistake or falls short? How many chances should he be given? I will examine this question both in terms of the systems that we use to manage and adjust performance across government; and in terms of my personal philosophy for tolerance of mistakes at an individual level.

The first level of monitoring consists of measuring performance according to a strategic plan. We use a comprehensive electronic system that encompasses thousands of performance indicators for measuring the achievements of ministries against their plans. That way, I myself can follow up on the performance of these ministries directly. Every minister can check his ministry's own indicators as well. We send reports to the different ministries on any shortcomings so that they can fix them as they occur.

The second level consists of field follow-up, which means monitoring the level of customer service. We have mystery shoppers and also customers who pay thousands of visits to ministries each year. They prepare reports on customer service that are raised to the concerned minister for review and are used to fix any shortcomings.

We too receive copies of these reports, but I do not base my decisions solely on them; hence the third level of monitoring, whereby I personally pay visits to government institutions. I follow up on their projects, check the successful models implemented at some government entities, and meet and listen to second-line and third-line managers. I do not believe in monitoring performance only from the office. Field monitoring gives a better idea of the levels of services and the implementation of policies, and therefore forms an important basis for practical decisions.

The fourth level of monitoring is financial, carried out by the State Audit Institution outside the government. Its reports are discussed at the highest government levels and sent to the concerned authorities to address deficiencies, if any.

" An exaggerated fear of mistakes stands in the way of creativity. "

The fifth level consists of a process managed by the Federal National Council. As this is external and carried out from a different perspective, it gives us new useful insights. We consider the recommendations of the Council and ratify the most relevant of these, for our goal is continually to improve and grow.

In the end, we all rally around one national vision – that of ensuring happiness and a decent life for our people.

To err is human and we all fall short in our work sometimes; but the most important thing is not to be negligent or make errors on purpose. This is the concept that guides our thinking when considering, for instance, how many chances to give an official before dismissing him.

It is by making mistakes that a person learns. If a person falls down, he does not get up where he has fallen, but rather a few steps ahead. Similarly, a person who errs will gain knowledge and experience as a result of his error. This does not mean that we go easy on mistakes, but that we allow some flexibility with loyal and hard-working officers for, I repeat: to err is human.

I might go easy on people who make mistakes, but never on people who make no effort. I do not like our officials to have an exaggerated fear of mistakes. That kind of fear stands in the way of creativity, innovation and change. A few mistakes made by a person working productively cost far less than a person paralysed by laziness or fear.

Sheikh Mohammed examines air traffic control systems at the Sheikh Zayed Air Navigation Centre in Abu Dhabi.

" Field monitoring gives a better idea of the levels of services and the implementation of policies, and therefore forms an important basis for practical decisions. "

Accession Day

25

Since I came to power in the Emirate of Dubai on 4 January 2006, this date has been commemorated each year as Accession Day. It was customary for people to celebrate Accession Day by publishing wishes and greetings in the media, decorating the streets, remembering past achievements, and organising receptions, parties and parades. I appreciate people's feelings and their desire to dedicate a day to this occasion every year. However, I thought about making some changes and rededicating this day instead to honour sections of society that deserve our attention and appreciation.

I love my people. God knows my appreciation for them and my true desire to serve them and to build a country that ensures their happiness. I am also confident of their feelings for me and their appreciation for what we are doing. But I have seen much energy, time and money spent on this day that could be much better used elsewhere in society. So in 2011 we came up with

"The fastest way to happiness is by instilling happiness in the hearts of others."

Sheikh Mohammed sits with orphans after taking them for a day out at the Bab Al Shams desert resort.

the idea of dedicating Accession Day to orphans, and we urged whoever wished to congratulate us through advertisements in the media to instead spend the same amount of money on orphans.

I met with a group of orphans in the care of the Ministry of Social Affairs and sent a message through them to the entire society: these orphans are my children, Sheikh Khalifa's children and the children of all Emirati people. Society responded to our appeal and many institutions ramped up their efforts to improve the lives of orphans. During the holy month of Ramadan last year, we launched a village for orphans to provide them with all the amenities and comfort they need, another idea born of Accession Day.

In 2012 we dedicated Accession Day to mothers. I personally launched a series of initiatives and visited a few families with mothers who successfully balance their work with motherhood, setting an example for their society through strength and patience.

I signed a thank you certificate, and asked every child to print it and present it to his or her mother. Over a million certificates were printed through my website, producing just the result we had intended.

This campaign has given me much more happiness than any other.

In 2013 we dedicated Accession Day to general labour staff – domestic workers, street cleaners, construction workers, public transportation drivers and others who make our lives easier and better every day, but who sometimes go completely unnoticed.

I was amazed at people's interaction with this campaign – children and adults, men and women. The celebrations extended over a month, during which tens of thousands of workers were honoured. The greatest satisfaction was seeing the smiles on their faces, and showing them that we value their services and are grateful for what they offer to our country.

Transforming this national occasion into an interactive social experience has turned out to be a great success. True happiness does not come from hanging a picture on a wall or publishing congratulations in newspapers, but from drawing a smile of satisfaction on a mother's face, or instilling a sense of security in an orphan, or by showing a worker that the whole society appreciates his or her services.

The fastest way to happiness is by instilling happiness in the hearts of others.

Sheikh Mohammed congratulates a municipal worker recognised as an 'unsung hero' as part of the Dubai Government Excellence Program Awards.

> " **True happiness comes from drawing a smile of satisfaction on a mother's face, or instilling a sense of security in an orphan, or by showing a worker that the whole society appreciates his or her services.** "

The UAE's success

26

During the dialogue session at the Government Summit, a foreign participant asked me the recipe of the UAE's success.

Success is not a destination, but a journey. Each time that you reach a summit on this journey, you must look ahead to the next one. So when I am asked to explain the secret of our country's success, I first point out that we are still on the road to success, since we have by no means achieved all we want. We will always be on the road to a greater success.

Still, it is worth reflecting on the qualities that have carried us so far on this journey, and in so short a time. Foremost among these qualities is love. By this I mean the love that each and every one of our people has for this country. Yes, we love the UAE.

Each year I encounter thousands of citizens in schools, in government centres, in business, in the streets and in malls, and I can see in their eyes the love they have for the UAE. I can feel their deep desire to serve their country and to raise its profile. Even expatriates, whom I also encounter in great numbers, are keen to contribute to the growth of this country that they sincerely love. Our people – be they engineers, doctors, teachers, soldiers, traders or government or private sector employees – care for the UAE as they would for their own children. They love the UAE as a child would his parents and are willing to sacrifice themselves for this country. Such strong feelings for our country influence any work we carry out, any project we undertake and any development to which we aspire. This is the foremost reason behind our success.

The second reason is our team spirit. Our president and rulers, the crown princes of Abu Dhabi and the other emirates, the ministers, and the federal and local government officials all work as a team. Everybody takes part in building the UAE. We inherited this spirit from our founding fathers and we uphold it still today.

It is not easy for a federation to work as one with local governments. We have seen many federations elsewhere in which local interests come into conflict with federal interests, but the UAE has proven to be an exception to this rule.

It is our team spirit, combined with the love we have for our country, that has given spirit to our Union, which in turn gives us strength, motivation and perseverance. As for the challenges that we face, they instil in us complete faith in our capabilities and those of our youth. This forward-looking, motivating and energetic spirit is the fruit of the efforts undertaken at the birth of our nation in 1971.

I still remember a proverb that I read in a book some time ago: "If you want luxury for one year, grow wheat; if you want luxury for a decade, grow trees; if you want luxury for a century, grow people."

" Success is not a destination, but a journey. Each time that you reach a summit on this journey, you must look ahead to the next one. "

Sheikh Khalifa chairs a meeting of the UAE Supreme Council on National Day, comprising Their Highnesses, the rulers of all seven emirates.

Foremost among the qualities behind the success of the UAE is the love that each and every one of our people has for this country. Yes, we love the UAE.

**" Working as a team,
everybody takes part in
building the UAE. "**

Aid to the world

27

The UAE has a proud record of providing assistance to people in other countries who find themselves afflicted, destitute or otherwise less fortunate than us. Since its inception in 1971, the UAE has provided an estimated 160 billion dirhams (around US$43 billion) in foreign aid. Annual foreign aid is equivalent to around one per cent of our gross national income. These figures place us at the forefront of foreign aid contributions worldwide.

It is against our customs and morals to brag about helping others, but still I feel the need to explain our approach to foreign aid and its catalysts, both for the record and also to set an example to other countries and to future generations.

Sheikh Zayed

It all started with the Father of our Nation. Sheikh Zayed is at the root of our generous nature and his name has become synonymous with true giving.

Sheikh Zayed does not need our testimony, for the cities of Palestine, the hills of Pakistan, the plains of Morocco and Egypt, the dams of Yemen, the villages of Bangladesh and many, many other places bear witness to his generosity. Even the Holy Land of Jerusalem and its surroundings bear witness to his good deeds.

It is Sheikh Zayed, God bless his soul, who instilled benevolence in our hearts, taught us the principles of giving, and accustomed us to doing good deeds.

Sheikh Khalifa

Generous by nature and compassionate at heart, such is our President, Sheikh Khalifa. It is no wonder that in one year, more than half of UAE foreign aid came from a single source, the Abu Dhabi Fund for Development, under the directives of Sheikh Khalifa. That fund alone contributed 4.9 billion dirhams (around US$1.3 billion) to UAE foreign aid in just one year, not to mention the Khalifa Foundation and other charities working directly under Sheikh Khalifa.

Perhaps the following verse best describes Sheikh Khalifa:

However you reach the sea,
You will find its depth filled with goodness,
And its shores lined with generosity.

" The UAE is not just a financial and economic nucleus, neither is it just a tourism hub: we are also a nerve centre of global humanitarian work. "

Philanthropy

The UAE takes pride in its great philanthropists, such as Sheikha Fatima bint Mubarak, God bless her, known as the 'Mother of the Nation' or the 'Mother of Giving'; and Sheikh Hamdan bin Zayed Al Nahyan (Ruler's Representative in the Western Region) among many others.

The country also embraces numerous charities and many anonymous humanitarians who are surely known to God. Philanthropy is in the roots of our culture.

The Emirati people do not live in luxury and isolation from the world around. On the contrary, we are a vibrant people, we empathise with the suffering of others. We contribute positively to alleviating their pain, helping those in need, and fighting poverty, hunger and sickness on earth.

We give without hesitation. When the global financial crisis struck the world in 2009 and many countries curbed their charitable and humanitarian donations, the UAE went against the tide and actually increased its foreign aid.

We believe that giving knows no limits. As such, 95 per cent of our aid is not recovered to avoid burdening the economies of less fortunate countries.

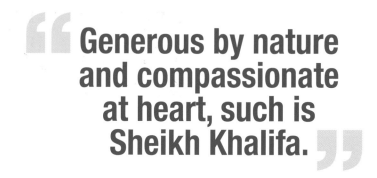

" Generous by nature and compassionate at heart, such is Sheikh Khalifa. "

We also give unconditionally. Our purpose is strictly humanitarian, untouched by political agendas, geographical boundaries or ethnic, racial or religious discrimination.

We strive to be an international humanitarian capital and a beacon of hope for all those in need. The UAE is not just a financial and economic nucleus, neither is it just a tourism hub: we are also a nerve centre of global humanitarian work.

We will always be there to lend a helping hand to our brothers and friends, and to the destitute and the needy, wherever they might be.

Such is our message to the world; such is the United Arab Emirates.

> **Sheikh Zayed is at the root of our generous nature and his name has become synonymous with true giving.**

28

I was asked by a government employee: "What do you expect from us?" My answer is that government employees are the main drivers of development. They are our true capital. We count on them for improving our services, achieving our vision, and delivering on the expectations of our people. A great vision can only be achieved by a great team.

The development of government is only possible through the development of its workforce. It is by nurturing creative employees that the entire government becomes creative. It is by equipping employees with new skills that the entire government is modernised. Our workforce is central to our government and as such, we are always sure to develop and train them to be the best they can be. Last year alone we invested more than 1.3 million hours in training more than 55,000 federal government employees.

We launched a leadership programme for second-line and third-line leaders, and gave out excellence awards to our employees, since competition among employees brings out the best in them. We replaced the criterion of seniority with the principle of competence in promotion and recruitment. Today it is competence and accomplishment that prevail.

I have three points of advice for public servants.

First, act like a leader, for true leadership is not in one's position, but in one's way of thinking and acting: it is in the nobility of one's objectives and goals. A true leader serves the people, acts in their interests and works for their happiness. A true leader does not need to be supervised in order to devote himself to his work, to achieve and to innovate. He should have an inner impetus that makes him aim for no less than first place.

A true leader does not derive power from his position, but from his ethics, from people's love for him, and from his knowledge, education and excellence in his field of work. To all government employees, I say this: You are all leaders, and therefore you should exceed all expectations.

" First, act like a leader, for true leadership is not in one's position, but in one's way of thinking and acting: it is in the nobility of one's objectives and goals. "

Second, if you look at civil service as a mere job, you will be a mere employee. You are a leader, not an employee, and this role is more than a job, it is also an opportunity. It is an opportunity to show your talents and capabilities, an opportunity to add new value to your society. It is an opportunity to inspire and influence all those around you. Even more, it is an opportunity to contribute to the making of your country's history. So do not carry out your work as an employee, but as a leader who loves his country, as a craftsman who is passionate about his craft, and as an artist who excels in his art. We expect no less from you.

Third, develop your capabilities continuously, expand your knowledge and broaden your horizon, and never give up on your work. Perseverance is much more important than intelligence. Any improvement on your work, no matter how minimal, could produce remarkable outcomes. So never stop developing yourself and never look back. Always aim at first place and at serving your country and society.

May God grant us all success in the service of our country and people, and in our mission to raise the profile of the UAE.

> **If you look at civil service as a mere job, you will be a mere employee.**

Sheikh Mohammed breaks fast with staff at Fujairah Hospital during the holy month of Ramadan.

" Do not carry out your work as an employee, but as a leader who loves his country, as a craftsman who is passionate about his craft, and as an artist who excels in his art. "

Motivating teams

29

During the Summit a government team leader asked me how we should motivate people to achieve better performance. This is an interesting topic to explore in more detail here. The first key to motivating a person toward better performance is to empower him or her to achieve. Nothing motivates an employee more than seeing the results of his own achievements. Granting power in this way is also an expression of trust and respect. I sometimes receive complaints in my personal email from employees who spend long years in their jobs without any real power, and therefore without any real achievements that they can call their own. So to my fellow officials I say: do not be afraid to give real power to your employees, because you too once stood in their shoes, and if you had not been given the power to achieve, you would not have arrived where you are today.

We must believe in the capabilities of our teams. Every person has tremendous capacities. A true leader is one who creates a favourable environment to bring out the energy and ability of his team. A great leader creates more great leaders, and does not reduce the institution to a single person. We sometimes look for second-line and third-line leaders in an institution, but find none, because the person in charge has not sufficiently empowered his team to bring out and refine their capacity for leadership.

The second key to motivation is the need to reward distinguished and creative employees. They should be held up as examples for the whole institution. Human competition is central to every aspect of our life. Even our religion requires us to compete in doing good deeds. You can never create a competitive environment unless you reward and praise creativity. Praising employees means giving credit for success to them, and not only to yourself. It means honouring their accomplishments and showing your belief that the success of the institution embodies the success of every single one of them. If employees see their leader attributing success to them rather than to himself, they will hold him in high esteem. They will regard him as their role model, not only as their leader.

The third driver of motivation is related to the idea with which this book began: that the job of the government is to ensure the happiness of society. Well, employees are part of this society, and so it is necessary to ensure their happiness in order that they in turn can bring happiness to others.

> **One's job is a major part of one's life, and life is too precious to spend in misery.**

A happy employee is more productive, more energetic and more creative – hence the importance of creating a happy environment within every institution. In order to make employees happy, we must show that we care about them, we must share in their joys and pains, we must help them to create balance in their lives, and we must add value and motivation to their jobs. Most importantly, we must listen attentively to what they have to say. A successful leader listens to his or her employees, for listening is an expression of respect and appreciation.

I hope that officials will work in this way to nurture their employees' happiness; for one's job is a major part of one's life, and life is too precious to spend in misery.

> **It is necessary to ensure employees' happiness in order that they in turn can bring happiness to others.**

Sheikh Mohammed speaks with UAE government leaders at a session of the Sheikh Khalifa Government Excellence Program.

> **A great leader creates more great leaders, and does not reduce the institution to a single person.**

One nation

30

Some people, both inside and outside this country, have misconceptions about the nature of the relationship between the UAE federal government and the local governments in each emirate, as well as the nature of the relationships among the emirates. Some imagine a conflict of interest or unhealthy competition, and a few foreign newspapers have even gone so far as to liken our situation to a cold war.

Those under such an illusion are obviously unaware of the nature of the relationship between the ruling families in the emirates. They have no idea of our history, of our vision for the future, of the character of our people, or of the ethics of our leaders. And the biggest problem is that they do not even know that they do not know!

We are one country with one constitution, one flag and one vision. We have one president, Sheikh Khalifa. What belongs to Abu Dhabi belongs to Dubai and the other emirates, just as what belongs to Dubai belongs to Abu Dhabi and the other emirates. All the local governments are proud of the achievements of our federal government, which in turn takes pride in the local achievements of every emirate.

We are not just emirates; we are the United Arab Emirates. All of our citizens share the same interests and priorities with Sheikh Khalifa, myself, the rulers of the emirates and the officials of their governments.

The Union was built to endure and thrive. The seeds sown by Sheikh Zayed, Sheikh Rashid and their fellow founding fathers have deep roots that are only strengthened by the passing of the years. We are one country because we feel such unity deep down, not because we signed some agreements in 1971. Every one of our citizens is willing to sacrifice himself to preserve every inch of our land.

Our local projects complement each other, while our federal government supports the country's development and growth by providing legislative and legal frameworks and international representation. Nevertheless, we all remain united around one pure vision: human development for every inch of this country.

The Government Summit that inspired this book was an example of exactly this spirit. It brought together officials from the federal government and every local government under one roof, to exchange information, expertise and successful experiences. This is what we seek: to work with one spirit, according to one vision.

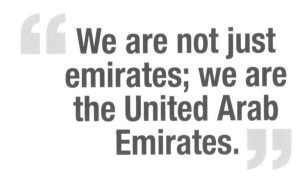

We are not just emirates; we are the United Arab Emirates.

To everyone working in federal and local governments, I say this: You are the drivers of our country's growth and development. Your work as one team is what wins us top positions worldwide. By improving processes, developing services and integrating policies, you will make the life of your fellow citizens easier, better and happier.

We have a vision to enable any citizen to complete any government transaction (federal or local) in any government authority (federal or local). We have tremendous potential, smart systems, creative minds, capable people and a strong political will to achieve this objective.

Our goal is to be among the best nations worldwide, because the Emirati people will settle for nothing less than the very best.

We are one country because we feel such unity deep down, not because we signed some agreements in 1971.

Sheikh Mohammed surveys Siji Dam in Central Region, an example of strategic investment in infrastructure by the UAE to support sustainable development across its territory.

No time to waste

31

When people remark on my constant rush to execute projects, I respond that the future starts today, not tomorrow. When people ask, "Why do you want everything now?", I answer, "Why not?" There is no point in waiting. If we wait until tomorrow we will forever procrastinate. So whenever we feel that a project will serve our people, develop our economy and advance our country, we undertake it without delay.

The UAE has transformed itself from an arid desert into a well-developed nation on the global stage in just four short decades. We have never had the luxury of time. We have never accustomed ourselves to waiting. We rush to execute development projects because we believe that a state with economic power also reaps the benefits of political power.

None of our country's achievements would have been possible without the efforts of work teams from every emirate, from Abu Dhabi to Fujairah; or without the participation of every one of our people, from the President to the lowest-ranking employee.

The future does not wait for hesitant people. The more we achieve, the more we realise how much more we can achieve.

Here I would like to recount a personal anecdote. I have got used to inviting the media to dinner each year after evening prayers during the holy month of Ramadan. At these times, we get the chance to discuss different social issues and developments. A few years ago during one of those dinners, a journalist came up to me and asked the following question: "How much of your vision have you achieved so far?" She wanted to know a percentage figure. I tried to dodge the question, but in vain. So after a moment of thought I told her that our ambitions were great, as were the expectations of our people, and that we had accomplished around 10 per cent of our vision.

A couple of years later, at the same time of year and in the same place, the same journalist came up to me and asked the same question. We had recently completed Burj Khalifa, launched Dubai Metro and inaugurated Meydan City, in addition to a host of other impressive projects. After pondering her question – she once again asked for a percentage – I answered that we had accomplished around seven per cent of our vision. Surprised, she exclaimed, "But your answer was 10 per cent a couple of years ago!" To which I replied, "Of course – for the greater our accomplishments, the wider our vision, the broader our horizons and the clearer our perception."

> **Our objective is to make our people happy and there is no delaying happiness. Multiply the days of delay by the number of people to calculate the years wasted in procrastination.**

This is a lifelong journey with no finish line. Each time we complete one phase, new possibilities unfold before our eyes. We will continue without halt or rest, for halting is a waste of time. We will pass on the torch for generations to come. We ask God to help us leave our mark on this country and to serve it as best as we can.

Returning to our topic, our objective is to make our people happy and there is no delaying happiness. Time is too precious to waste on postponing our people's dreams and expectations. You just have to multiply the days of delay by the number of people to calculate the years wasted in procrastination. Why waste millions of days of our people's lives in hesitation and waiting? Why defer our people's luxury, happiness and comfort?

They say that rushing is a quality of successful leaders because their time is precious. Well, I say that rushing is a quality of successful nations that give due importance to time and due credit to the passing days.

A successful nation forges its own path to success without relying on the situation around it. A successful nation does not wait for the future, but rolls up its sleeves and makes the future. A successful nation does not put off today's work for tomorrow, but starts tomorrow's work today.

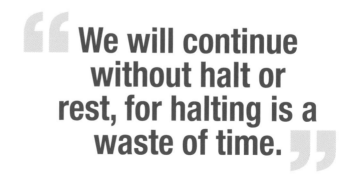

We will continue without halt or rest, for halting is a waste of time.

Sheikh Khalifa, Sheikh Mohammed and Sheikh Mohammed bin Zayed (Crown Prince of Abu Dhabi), stand before a field of solar panels at the inauguration of Shams 1, the world's largest concentrated solar power plant. Shams 1 is a project of Abu Dhabi's Masdar sustainable energy initiative.

" The future starts today, not tomorrow. "

Family tourism

32

Every year the UAE welcomes more than 10 million tourists from all around the world. We have a highly successful tourism industry which has grown into a key pillar of our national economy.

Many years ago we focused on a new kind of tourism: family tourism. First, we launched Dubai Shopping Festival in 1996 to offer a unique tourist experience to all family members. This annual festival has proved to be a huge success: today its direct economic returns are estimated at 15 billion dirhams (around US$4 billion) per year.

The past few years have also seen the construction of many significant attractions in our country as well as the expansion of Emirates Airline. Hence, the UAE has become a major international destination for family tourism all year round.

I am overjoyed to see Gulf and Arab families strolling around our cities. Our feelings towards tourists from within this region are like family ties. After all, we are brothers and sisters, and a person cannot help but be happy to see his near and dear ones. Needless to say, visitors from all parts of the world are also our most welcome friends and guests.

Some time ago we instructed all government authorities to pay special attention to family tourism by providing adequate facilities, accommodation and programmes.

We aim to be part of the special memories of our brothers and sisters in Gulf and Arab countries, and we welcome them with a warm heart and open arms, wishing them prosperity and stability.

Each country has its own unique experiences from which the whole world can benefit. That is why we make it our business not only to set an example to other countries, but also to learn from each and every one of them. We are not fishing for compliments, for we know exactly where the UAE stands. What pleases us most is when our mistakes and weaknesses are pointed out to us.

I wish happiness, prosperity and stability for all Arab countries. Our region possesses all the right ingredients for developing its tourism industry. It also abounds in treasures that should be better exploited. It is the starting point of history, the cradle of civilisations and the heart of religions. It is endowed with the most beautiful and diverse climate all year round. It has the richest history and heritage, and the tastiest cuisines in the world.

" Our region abounds in touristic treasures that should be better exploited. "

What more can a tourist ask for, other than a few simple service facilities?

Stability and development in the Arab region are the keys to progress for its people, not only in tourism but also in industry, agriculture, energy, sciences and knowledge. Today, it grieves me to see the unrest and tension in our region. I pray to God to help us restore our glory and standing, and to grant our people success and prosperity.

> **Our feelings towards tourists from within the Gulf and Arab region are like family ties. After all, we are brothers and sisters, and a person cannot help but be happy to see his near and dear ones.**

Sheikh Mohammed speaks with an exhibitor at the Arabian Travel Market in 2012. Also pictured (far left) is Sheikh Ahmed bin Saeed, Chairman of Emirates Group.

"We aim to be part of the special memories of our brothers and sisters in Gulf and Arab countries."

33

Whoever asks the question "Is leadership inherent or acquired?" has already taken his or her first step on the path to leadership. Leadership is a combination of intelligence, resourcefulness, wisdom, a strong personality and aspiration to the greatest of things. Most of these qualities are innate and hereditary, while some can also be acquired. However, even those who are born with such qualities must refine them through education, practice and communication in order to become successful leaders.

Leadership is neither conferred by chance at birth, nor guaranteed by study even at the finest academies. I personally know many graduates from such academies who have worked on themselves and expanded their knowledge to reach high leadership positions, while others stopped at some point because their qualities and skills did not help them to progress any further.

We have seen that an enquiring nature places some people ahead of others on the path to leadership. We also want to change the concept of leadership so that it includes anyone who has the ambition and the will to change himself, and also to benefit his society.

When we say 'leader', people tend to imagine political, military or historical figures who have changed the history of their peoples and countries. They may also imagine successful economic leaders who have transformed companies or given life to new creations and inventions. The hereditary qualities of those people, combined with their environment and their great self-development efforts, have made them exceptional leaders and enabled them to transform their societies and peoples.

But today, the concept of leadership is much more far-reaching. Anyone who can improve the life of those around him is a leader. Similarly, anyone who can serve people and make them happy is a leader. A leader is also a person capable of creating positive change, whether at work or at home, and of innovating and creating even the simplest of things. A leader excels in his craft, art, talent or profession.

All people are born with the seeds of such qualities, which they can nurture and grow, so that bit by bit, they advance on the path to leadership and ultimately evolve into great leaders.

"We want to change the concept of leadership so that it includes anyone who has the ambitions and the will to change himself, and also to benefit his society."

Every single achievement you make, every single life you change and every single skill you acquire brings you one step closer to becoming a better leader. Every day you can improve the leader in you to become a better person and a greater leader.

Were we to limit leadership to exceptional political, economic and scientific figures, we would confine such a vast field to a very limited circle of human beings. Everything can be learnt and every person is capable of self-development. Human development requires entire generations of leaders to lift up their nations and peoples.

A great vision needs not only a great leader, but also a great work team with diverse leadership qualities.

Looking at leadership from this perspective, there is no need to ask whether it is inherent or acquired, but rather whether one wants to become a leader or not.

" Every single achievement you make, every single life you change and every single skill you acquire brings you one step closer to becoming a better leader. "

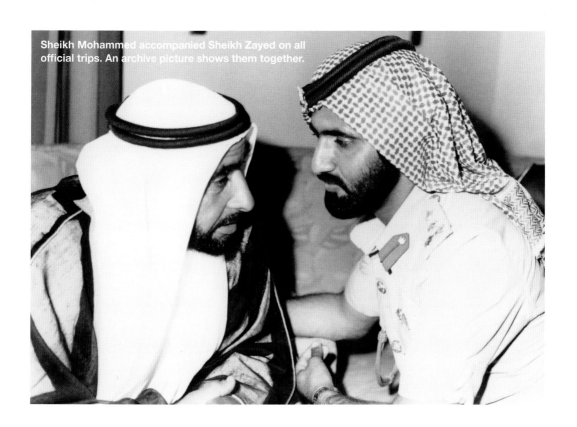

Sheikh Mohammed accompanied Sheikh Zayed on all official trips. An archive picture shows them together.

"Leadership is a combination of intelligence, resourcefulness, wisdom, a strong personality and aspiration to the greatest of things."

Cabinet reshuffle

34

During the Government Summit that inspired this book, a reporter, who is also a friend, asked how satisfied I was with the development of government performance, and whether I intended to reshuffle my government in the near future. Of course his question was not 100 per cent innocent – not with all the ministers and media present at the dialogue session.

I started by talking about developments in government performance and the extent of my satisfaction with them. There is no denying that the UAE has reached high rankings worldwide on a range of important measures, such as developing infrastructure and technology, providing an open investment environment and enabling the speedy completion of many kinds of transactions. We have taken strides forward in foreign commercial and diplomatic relations, the empowerment of women, security and safety, and various other fields where the government has collaborated with other partners to pen great success stories for the whole country.

At the same time, there is no doubt that some sectors such as education, health and Emiratisation need ongoing development, and we have made sure to place these at the top of our priority list for the coming phase of government.

We constantly encourage government officials to achieve more. We continuously offer opportunities in training, development, and the exchange of knowledge and expertise, both locally and abroad. We give officials one chance after another to develop themselves – but not indefinitely. There comes a time when we have to thank an official for his work and give someone else a chance to pump new blood into our institutions. Such is life, and such is the business of government.

Only achievers who are able to keep up with change, take on challenges and bring out the best in their teams will stay. Only innovative and creative officials with wide horizons, great determination, positive energy and optimism will stay. Every official knows himself, and ultimately it is the people who bear witness to his achievements. Therefore, I should not be the one to judge. Let them be accountable to themselves, and to the people, for their actions.

Our founding father, Sheikh Zayed, God bless his soul, used to say, "People will eventually depart, and money will not last forever, but our country will remain, and so will the work we carry out for our country."

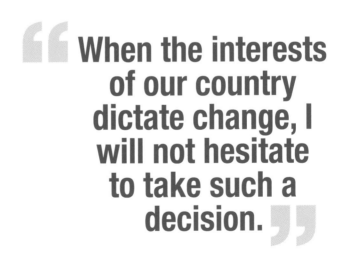

When the interests of our country dictate change, I will not hesitate to take such a decision.

So, to those who would like to leave their mark on this country I say, "The stage is yours." To those who seek personal glory I say, "You have condemned yourself to oblivion."

As to the question of change in government, I always repeat that when the interests of our country dictate change, I will not hesitate to take such a decision. Our objective is not change per se, but changing for the better. If we can achieve this with the same team, so much the better. If we cannot, then we will consider changing the team.

> **Our objective is not change per se, but changing for the better. If we can achieve this with the same team, so much the better. If we cannot, then we will consider changing the team.**

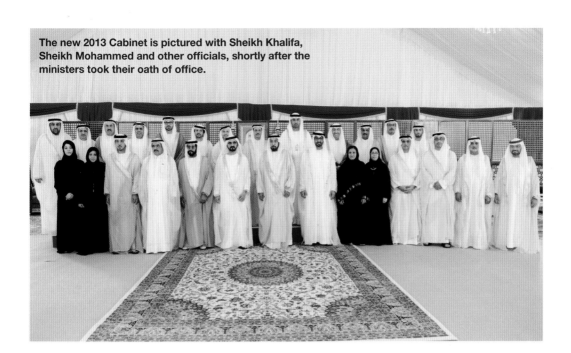

The new 2013 Cabinet is pictured with Sheikh Khalifa, Sheikh Mohammed and other officials, shortly after the ministers took their oath of office.

> " To those who would like to leave their mark on this country I say, 'The stage is yours.' "

A child's dream

35

During the dialogue session, I was impressed by a child who asked me in all innocence and courage how he could become a horseman like me.

I told him that by asking this question, he had already taken the first step on the right path, for it is said that questions account for half of one's knowledge. Horse riding is not just a sport; it represents high morals, nobility, chivalry and excellence. Horse riding starts from the inside.

I told this child that the first lesson in horse riding is that he should love and obey his parents, excel at school, respect his elders and possess a horseman's qualities of vigour and chivalry among others. It is only when he acquires such attributes and when his parents, his teachers and the people around him are satisfied with his high morals, that the easier part of learning how to ride a horse in clubs and other training facilities can follow.

A child's love for horse riding expresses his high ambitions and great determination. I always encourage our little ones to ride, for I have seen the great influence of this sport on them. Some 1400 years ago, Omar ibn Al Khattab, one of the four Righteous Caliphs in Islam, observed: "Teach your children swimming, archery and horseback riding." He was an Arab horseman, a wise leader and one of the greatest figures in history. So for him to advise of horse riding did not come out of nowhere; it rather establishes a solid relationship of horse riding to dignity, pride, chivalry and high morals.

Horse riding embodies a strong bond between the horseman and his horse, as well as a synchronisation between the horseman's movements and the horse's progression. It teaches the horseman patience, strength, control and speed – qualities that should grow in our children. Inner morals harmonise with outer qualities, just as self-confidence harmonises with speed of movement and strength. The force of the emotions that bond the horseman to his horse is reflected in the qualities of endurance and patience that develop.

The relationship of Emirati people to horses comes from our authentic Arab roots and this perpetuates the sport of our ancestors. Today, horse riding represents our Arab and Islamic identity, our pride in our heritage and our high morals, which we are instilling in our younger generations. Only goodness comes from horses; as the Prophet, peace be upon him, said: "Goodness is tied to the forelocks of horses until the Day of Resurrection." Horse riding is an everlasting sport. Only good people treat horses with kindness and only great spirits seek and practice horse riding.

> **Only good people treat horses with kindness and only great spirits seek and practice horse riding.**

36

During the dialogue session, I was asked if there is any link between leadership and taking part in sports. My reply was, "Can you imagine a lazy or inactive leader?" A leader should be fit, healthy and athletic. He should be both mentally and physically active. He must have a strong build and a sharp mind. Hence I say, 'a sound leader in a sound body'.

Personally, sports are an essential part of my daily schedule. If I am not fully energetic and healthy myself, I will not be able to get my team moving. Not only do sports develop your body muscles, they build your mind's muscles as well. I walk no less than three kilometres a day, 10 kilometres once a week, and 20 kilometres once a fortnight. Besides walking regularly, I practice different hobbies such as horse riding and cycling. My daily workout does not hinder my productivity in any way, since I carry out my work over the phone while exercising.

My advice to all is to practice sports on a regular basis, for the quality of your life is related to the quality of your health, and your level of achievement in life depends on how energetic and active you feel. It is said that health is a treasure; well, I say that if time is life, then health gives meaning to our time and adds spice to life.

It bothers me to hear, watch and read about the many cases of cardiovascular disease, hypertension and diabetes due to lack of exercise. Our modern life of luxury offers all sorts of treats and delights. Our ancestors did not suffer from the

sound body

diseases which are widespread today, and the main reason was their active life and the nature of their work.

I sometimes encounter groups of women out walking for exercise. I am so overjoyed to see this that I stop a few moments to encourage them to keep up this good habit, and exchange a few words. I was once speaking about these moments and the importance of workouts and self-discipline in eating. The person I was talking to replied that he personally could not resist food and neither could he

> **"Those who have control over themselves can control the world around them, unlike those who do not have self-control."**

commit himself to working out. I replied, "Those who have control over themselves can control the world around them, unlike those who do not have self-control."

Some make their busy schedule an excuse for not working out; I wonder of what use their money will be to them if their health fails. Others give researching, learning and reading as an excuse; I wonder if their education will be any good to them without good health. Nothing in your life, not even the quality time you spend with your family, could be complete without good health.

And so, I end with the simplest of advice: make time in your life for exercise, for this is the soundest investment that can be made in health, future and happiness.

> **" If time is life, then health gives meaning to our time and adds spice to life. "**